LEGO

Animal Atlas

Written by Rona Skene

DK | Penguin Random House

Senior Editor Rona Skene
Project Art Editor Jenny Edwards
Pre-Production Producer Siu Yin Chan
Producer Louise Daly
Managing Editor Paula Regan
Managing Art Editor Jo Connor
Art Director Lisa Lanzarini
Publisher Julie Ferris
Publishing Director Simon Beecroft

Inspirational models built by Jason Briscoe,
Rod Gillies, and Simon Pickard
Animals consultant Cathriona Hickey
Builds consultant Simon Hugo
Maps built by Jenny Edwards, James McKeag,
and Elena Jarmoskaite
Photography by Gary Ombler
Additional design by James McKeag, Elena
Jarmoskaite, Gema Salamanca, and Rhys Thomas

Dorling Kindersley would like to thank Randi Sørensen,
Heidi K. Jensen, Paul Hansford, Martin Leighton Lindhardt,
Melody Louise Caddick, Mette Jørgensen, and Monika
Bukhave Fruergaard of the LEGO Group.

First American Edition, 2018
Published in the United States by DK Publishing
345 Hudson Street, New York, New York 10014
Page design copyright © 2018 Dorling Kindersley Limited
DK, a Division of Penguin Random House LLC

18 19 20 21 22 10 9 8 7 6 5 4 3 2 1
001–307933–June/18

Published in Great Britain by Dorling Kindersley Limited.

A catalog record for this book is available from the
Library of Congress.

ISBN: 978-1-4654-7494-0

DK books are available at special discounts when
purchased in bulk for sales promotions, premiums,
fund-raising, or educational use.
For details, contact: DK Publishing Special Markets,
345 Hudson Street, New York,
New York 10014.
SpecialSales@dk.com

Printed and bound in China

**A WORLD OF IDEAS:
SEE ALL THERE IS TO KNOW**

www.LEGO.com
www.dk.com

CONTENTS

Useful bricks

All LEGO® bricks are useful, but when you are making animals, some come in handy again and again. Don't worry if you don't have all these parts. Look at what you do have and let your creativity run wild!

Brick basics

Bricks are the basis of most LEGO builds. They come in many shapes and sizes, and are named according to size.

2x3 brick overhead view

2x3 brick side view

Plates are the same as bricks, only slimmer. Three stacked plates are the same height as a standard brick.

1x2 plate

3 plates

1x2 brick

Tiles look like plates, but without any studs on top. This gives them a smooth look for more realistic builds.

2x2 tile

2x2 round tile

1x6 tile

Slopes are any bricks with diagonal angles. They can be big, small, curved, or inverted (upside-down).

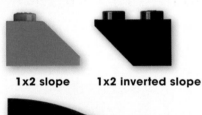

1x2 slope

1x2 inverted slope

1x3 curved slope

Cool connectors

Jumper plates allow you to "jump" the usual pattern of LEGO studs. They are great for centering things like noses.

1x2 jumper plate

There are different kinds of **bricks with side studs**. They all allow you to build outward as well as upward.

1x1 brick with two side studs

1x4 brick with side studs

Plates with balls and **plates with sockets** link together to make flexible joints that can be put into realistic poses.

Ball joint socket

2x2 brick with ball joint

Any piece with a bar can fit onto a **plate with a clip**. Use a **plate with a bar** and a clip to make a moving joint.

1x2 plate with bar

1x1 plate with clip

Hinge plates can give your builds side-to-side movement. **Hinge bricks** are used to tilt things up and down.

Hinge plates

1x2 hinge brick with 2x2 hinge plate

This **2x2 plate with a ring of bars** is a great starting point when building animals with lots of limbs!

Eyes

1x1 printed tile

1x1 round plate

1x1 round plate with hole

Headlight brick

Teeth

1x1 tooth plate

1x2 tooth plate

Noses

Flower plate

Jumper plate

1x1 angled tooth plate

1x1 cone

1x1 slope

Ears

2x2 round tile

1x1 plate with ring

Tongues

Minifigure lasso

Plant piece

Antennae

Joystick

Bar

Feet

Minifigure flipper

1x1 plate with side clip

Beaks

Horn piece

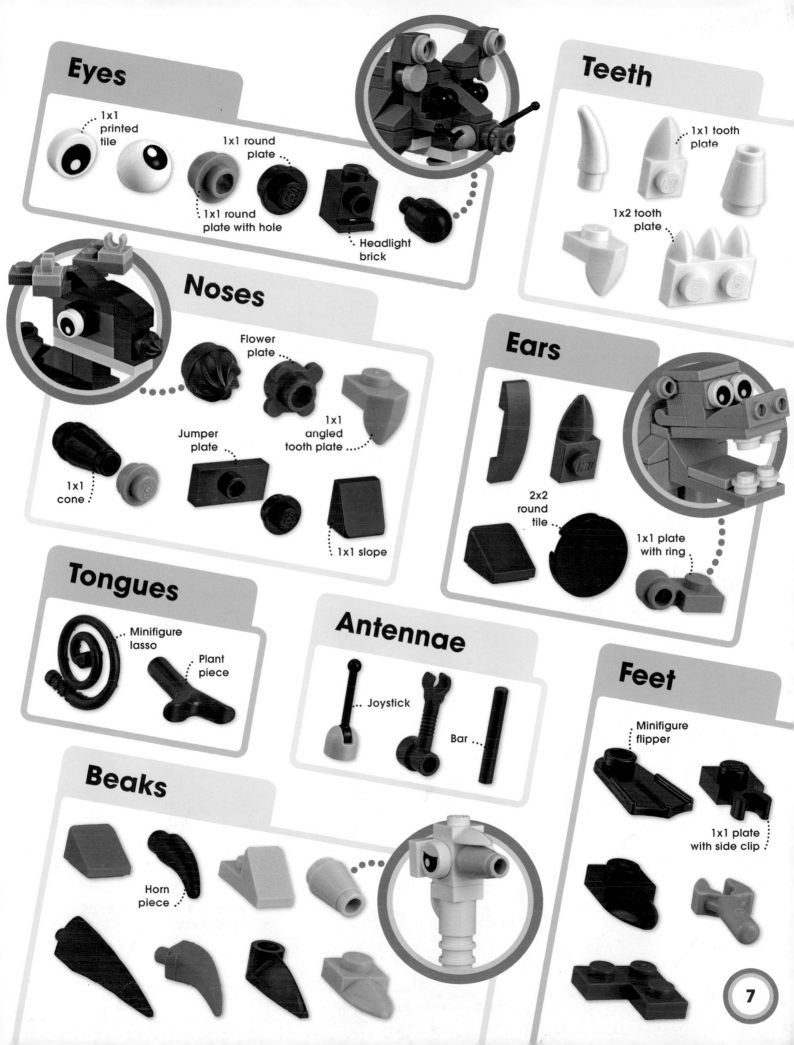

7

Build basics

Animals come in all shapes and sizes, and so do LEGO® builds. You can make an elephant that will fit in your hand, or a mouse as big as a house! Think about scale before you start on a new LEGO animal adventure.

Microbuilds

It's always fun to build big, but the best LEGO builders can also make something amazing with just a few bricks. The key to a cool microbuild is to choose a few **key features** of an animal and really make them stand out. In the case of this zebra, that's stripes, ears, and a tail!

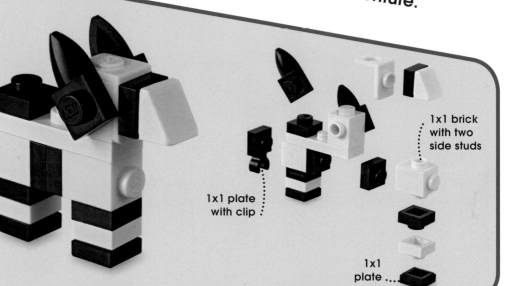

1x1 brick with two side studs

1x1 plate with clip

1x1 plate

Build tip!

Organize your bricks
Save time by organizing your bricks into colors and types before you start building.

Simple builds

Most of your LEGO animal builds will probably be big enough to have eyes, ears, and mouths. Choosing the right facial features will give even a simple build **lots of character**—as will fun extra details like this chimp's banana!

1x2/2x2 angled plate

Be creative
If you don't have the perfect piece, find a creative solution! Look for a different piece that can create a similar effect.

Build tip!

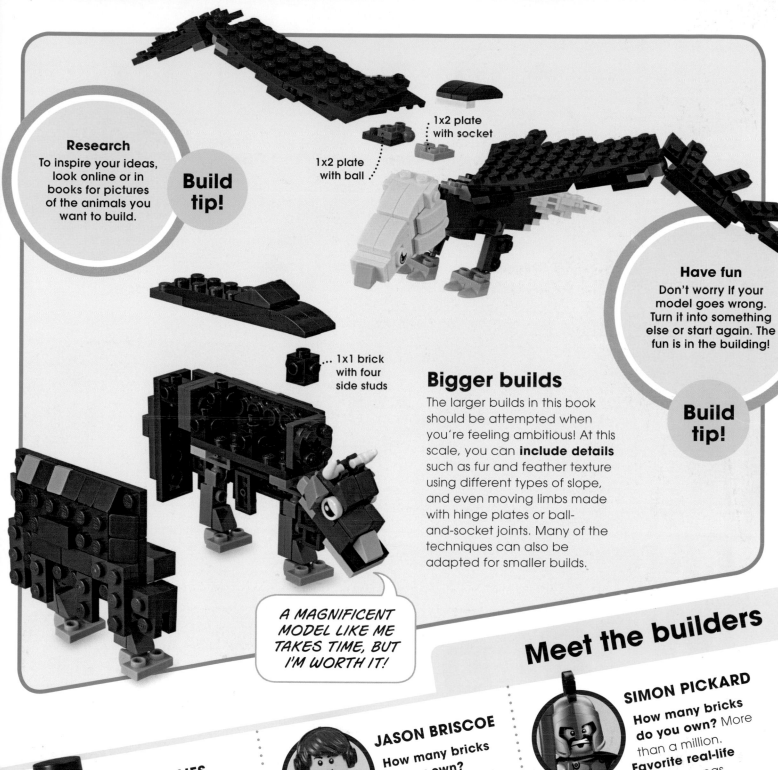

Research
To inspire your ideas, look online or in books for pictures of the animals you want to build.

Build tip!

1x2 plate with socket

1x2 plate with ball

Have fun
Don't worry If your model goes wrong. Turn it into something else or start again. The fun is in the building!

Build tip!

... 1x1 brick with four side studs

Bigger builds
The larger builds in this book should be attempted when you're feeling ambitious! At this scale, you can **include details** such as fur and feather texture using different types of slope, and even moving limbs made with hinge plates or ball-and-socket joints. Many of the techniques can also be adapted for smaller builds.

A MAGNIFICENT MODEL LIKE ME TAKES TIME, BUT I'M WORTH IT!

Meet the builders

ROD GILLIES
How many bricks do you own? Thousands and thousands!
Favorite real-life animals Sharks—they're so cool.
Favourite animal build in the book The tarantula. I'm scared of spiders in real life, so I was proud of myself for making a big, mean spider look goofy and cute!
Favorite brick The headlight, because it's so useful.

JASON BRISCOE
How many bricks do you own? About 2 million!
Favorite real-life animals Big cats, because they're so beautiful, and they need our protection.
Favorite animal build in the book The octopus—he was a real challenge, but I loved the result!
Favorite brick The macaroni tube, because it's super useful—just look at my octopus on page 67!

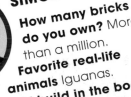

SIMON PICKARD
How many bricks do you own? More than a million.
Favorite real-life animals Iguanas.
Favorite animal build in the book The orangutan. He looks realistic but cute, and I was pleased with how I got him to cling to the tree!
Favorite brick The Dalek, because of its resemblance to the Dr. Who baddie! It's a 1x1 brick with studs all around it.

North America

Arctic Circle
This line shows the start of the northern polar region, which is the cold area around the North Pole.

FIND OUT ABOUT BUSY BEES ON PAGE 52!

ATLANTIC OCEAN

PACIFIC OCEAN

THE WORLD

South America

Equator
This imaginary line goes around the center of the Earth. Areas near the Equator are very hot.

ATLANTIC OCEAN

Animals live in almost every part of the world's continents and oceans. Each region has its own weather conditions, which we call its climate. Most animals prefer a specific kind of climate, but some, such as mice, can live almost anywhere.

MEET ME AND MY ANTARCTIC BUDDIES ON PAGE 72!

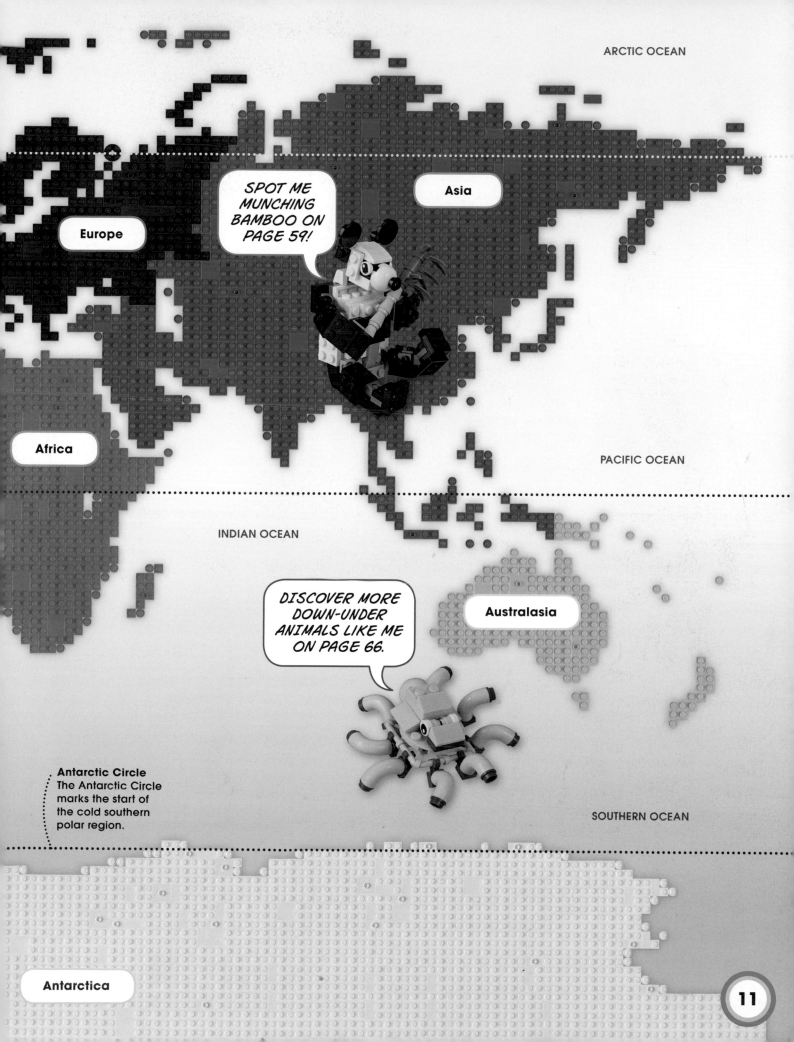

HABITATS

A habitat is a place where an animal can find all the things it needs to live. Animals can change the way they live or even how they look to survive in the habitat they live in. Here are just a few of the amazing habitats found on Earth.

Toucan

I'M A RAIN FOREST FAN. I LIKE MY FORESTS HOT AND STEAMY!

A COLD, SNOWY FOREST IS MY IDEA OF A PERFECT HOME!

Reindeer

▲ Forest

More animals live in forests than in any other habitat. There are two main kinds of forest: hot, humid **rain forests** near the Equator and cold, **coniferous forests** near the Arctic.

Barn owl

LIVING IN THE SAVANNA IS GREAT, APART FROM THE HUNGRY LIONS...

Zebra

▲ Woodland

Woodland areas have **four seasons**: spring, summer, fall, and winter. Trees grow new leaves in the spring and lose them in the fall. Woodlands are also called temperate forests.

▲ Grassland

These places have enough rainfall for **grasses to grow**, but not enough for trees. Grasslands can be hot, like the African savanna, or cool, like the North American prairies.

▲ Desert

Deserts are places that get less than 10 in (25 cm) of rain a year. Most deserts are **very hot**, but the icy continent of Antarctica counts as a desert, too!

Camel

▲ Wetland

Wetlands are soggy, **swampy areas** of land. They are a rich, food-filled environment for many water-loving plants and animals.

Alligator

FOR ME, HAPPINESS IS A WARM, SHALLOW CORAL REEF!

Clownfish

▲ Water

Watery habitats include freshwater **rivers and lakes**, as well as salty **seas and oceans**. All kinds of fish, birds, mammals, and insects make their homes in or near water.

Kangaroo

▲ Scrubland

Scrublands have **long, dry summers** and mild, wetter winters. The few plants that grow here are so tough that they can even withstand summer wildfires!

Guanaco

Polar bear

▲ Mountains

The high life is often harsh, with hardly any shelter from **strong sun or bitter winds**. Mountain animals and plants definitely have to be tough to survive!

▲ Snow and ice

The polar regions are the **coldest on Earth**, but that doesn't put off some wildlife! Plants are scarce, so most animals are carnivores (meat-eaters), like the polar bear.

Where in the world?

NORTH AMERICA

From raccoons to rattlesnakes and bears to bald eagles, North America is full of amazing animal life. The continent stretches from icy northern seas to hot, humid swamps in the south, with massive mountains, rocky deserts, and wide, grassy plains in between.

I CAN SWIM, CLIMB, AND RUN. I'D DEFINITELY WIN AN ANIMAL TRIATHLON!

I'M A MUSICAL MAMMAL! THE SOUND OF MY SONGS CARRIES FOR MILES UNDERWATER.

Bison

Coyote

Sea lion

Manatee

Humpback whale

Alligator

Black bear

Bald eagle

Skunk

Vulture

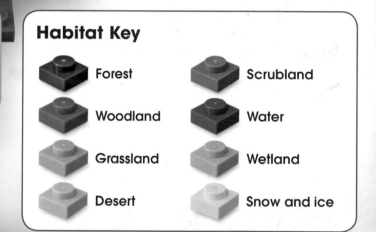

Record breakers

The world's **smallest bird** is the bee hummingbird from Cuba. It weighs just 0.03 oz (1 g)—about the same as a peanut!

The **monarch butterfly** can fly an incredible 2,000 miles (3,200 km) from Canada to Mexico to find winter food and warmth.

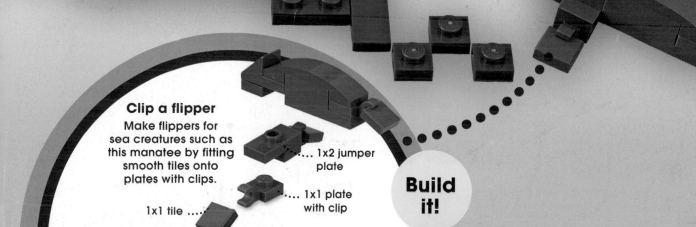

> WILY COYOTES LIKE ME WILL EAT ALMOST ANYTHING—EVEN TRASH FROM YOUR BINS!

Habitat Key

Forest		Scrubland	
Woodland		Water	
Grassland		Wetland	
Desert		Snow and ice	

Clip a flipper
Make flippers for sea creatures such as this manatee by fitting smooth tiles onto plates with clips.

···· 1x2 jumper plate

···· 1x1 plate with clip

1x1 tile ····

Build it!

Wild, wide grasslands

The huge, flat, grass-covered area in the middle of North America is called the prairies. It is home to many herbivores (plant-eating animals)—and the carnivores (meat-eaters) who hunt them!

Coyote ▼

Coyotes are wild members of the dog family. They live in big, noisy packs, using howls, growls, yelps, and barks to communicate with each other.

Coyotes have super-sharp hearing

Legs can run at 40mph (64 kph)

STEP AWAY OR I'LL SPRAY!

Smelly blast can hit a victim 3 m (10 ft) away

SHH! DON'T TELL, BUT I'M NOT REALLY A DOG! I'M A TYPE OF SQUIRREL.

Skunk ▶

When a skunk is in danger, it turns around and unleashes a secret weapon from under its tail—a stinky, oily spray directed straight at its enemy!

Habitat facts

The soil of the prairies is **very rich**, so most of it is now farmland. Only 1 percent of prairie land is still in its wild state.

Prairie grasses are tough. They **can survive** extreme weather and grazing animals. Even fire doesn't destroy them!

Prairie dogs stand upright to watch for danger

▲ Prairie dog

On flat land, the safest place for prairie dogs is underground, away from predators. Prairie dogs live together in huge burrows that have more than 50 entrances.

Thick coat grows in winter

I'M SO BIG THAT EVEN WOLF PACKS DON'T DARE TO TAKE ME ON!

◀ Bison

It takes a lot of grass to keep a beast as big as a bison going! That's why these huge, hairy cousins of the cow need to graze for more than 10 hours a day.

Hooves dig in snow for food

Build it!

A sideways look
The vulture's neck is built out sideways from an angle plate. The pieces turn upright again on a brick with a side stud.

1x2/2x2 angled plate

Sideways brick with side stud

Head has few feathers

◀ Jackrabbit

Long ears twitch at the sound of danger

Jackrabbits eat at night, when it's easier to hide from hungry hunters. When they sense danger, they take off on their long legs at speeds of 40 mph (64 kph).

PEOPLE CALL ME A SCAVENGER, BUT I PREFER TO SAY I'M A RECYCLER!

YIKES! A COYOTE AND A VULTURE? I'M OUT OF HERE!

▲ Vulture

Vultures are meat-eaters, but they don't usually kill prey. Instead, they cruise the skies, scanning the ground for already-dead animals. When they spot one, they swoop down and dig in!

Build it!

Jack's back
The jackrabbit's smooth back is made from curved slopes, with a clip where the head fits on.

1x2 plate with end bar

1x2 plate with top clip

17

Hot and steamy swamps

Wetlands are places where the land is waterlogged, or covered with shallow water. In Florida, the Everglades is a warm, watery wonderland for thousands of different swamp-loving animals.

Blue heron ▼
The heron patiently waits in the water for a fish to swim past. Then it darts its head down and snatches the prey with its sharp, pointed beak.

Flexible neck

Long, slim legs for wading

▼ Rattlesnake
When this snake senses danger, it shakes its tail, making a rattling noise. Then, it coils its body, ready to deliver a venomous bite.

I'M NORTH AMERICA'S LONGEST SNAKE, YOU KNOW!

Forked tongue is used for "smelling" prey

Manatee ▼
The manatee is also called the sea cow, because of the way it calmly grazes on sea grasses, looking a little like a cow in a field.

Build it!

1x2 plate with clips

1x2 plate with bar

2x2 slide plate

Tale of a tail
The manatee's tail is built with a hinge made from two plates so it can move up and down. It has a smooth slide plate underneath.

Thick layer of protective skin

Large tail flaps to push body through water

MY CLOSEST LAND RELATIVE IS THE MOUSE. OK, I'M KIDDING... IT'S THE ELEPHANT!

Eyes on stalks

Ball with printed eye

Sideways 1x4 curved slope

Plate with ring

The crab's eyes are built on plates with rings, built onto other plates with rings!

Build it!

Raccoon ▼

Raccoons are members of the bear family. These adaptable animals eat insects, eggs, fish, fruit, lizards, or leftover human food. In fact there's practically nothing they won't eat!

Black eye markings look like a mask

STAY AWAY FROM MY BURROW OR YOU'LL FEEL THE PINCH!

WATCH OUT—I CAN OPEN YOUR DOORS WITH MY NIMBLE FINGERS!

Strong claws for carrying food and fighting

.... Crabs can grow new legs to replace damaged ones

Habitat facts

The Everglades is the only place on Earth where you can find **crocodiles and alligators** living in the same habitat.

The most common plant in the Everglades is sawgrass. Its edges are **so sharp** that they can cut through your clothes!

▲ Blue land crab

Also called the giant land crab, this speedy scuttler will make a meal of almost anything near its burrow—leaves, fruit, insects, or even other crabs!

ALL THAT SNAPPING MEANS THAT I'LL GET THROUGH 3,000 TEETH IN MY LIFETIME!

▼ Alligator

Alligators hunt by lying still in water, with only their eyes and nostrils showing above the surface. Then—snap! They grab the prey in their jaws and swallow it whole.

Armor-plated skin

Razor-sharp teeth ......

Pacific ocean shores

In north-western North America, forest-covered mountains sweep down to meet the Pacific—the biggest, deepest ocean on our planet. The cool waters, rocky shores, and giant trees are home to an awesome variety of wildlife.

Pelican ▶

When the pelican flies over a school of fish, it plunges into the water. Its huge beak has a pouch of super-stretchy skin under it, perfect for scooping up lots of fish at once.

> I CAN WEIGH AS MUCH AS 600 OF YOU HUMANS!

◀ Humpback whale

Although the humpback is huge, it can jump right out of the water and land with a great splash! Even experts don't know exactly why. Maybe it's just for fun!

Blowholes for breathing air

Tail fins are called flukes

Smooth skin for faster swimming

Swordfish ▲

You can see how this fish got its name! Its long, pointed bill catches prey, and also makes a streamlined shape to help the swordfish swim super-fast.

Build it!

Making a point

The swordfish's eyes and sharp nose are built around a sideways brick with side studs.

Samurai sword

1x1 cone

1x1 brick with four side studs

Word on the wing

Build an impressive butterfly wing by stacking different-colored plates. Add small slopes and curved plates to make realistic edges.

1x1 slope

1x2 curved slope

Build it!

▼ Monarch butterfly

At the end of summer, many monarchs head south to sunny California or Mexico. They spend the winter roosting together in eucalyptus and pine trees.

Antennae sniff out sweet nectar

HOPE I REACH THE FISH BEFORE THAT PESKY BEAR GETS HIS PAWS ON IT!

Huge wings for maximum flying power

Fearsome hooked beak

◄ Bald eagle

A hunter such as the bald eagle is called a bird of prey. When it spies a fish, it swoops down, grabs the prey in its huge claws and flies to a safe place to dig into its fishy meal.

Black bear ►

Black bears make their home in the forests that hug the coastline. They look fierce, but these bears mainly eat roots and berries, with just the occasional fish.

Huge, powerful paws

Habitat facts

The coast redwood is the **tallest tree** in the world. It can grow to 350 ft (107 m) tall. That's as high as a 30-story building!

Seaweed is one of the reasons this area is so rich in wildlife. **Undersea forests** provide food for many different plants and animals.

◄ Sea lion

Sea lions live in big, noisy groups along the rocky ocean shore. Their bodies are the ideal shape for swimming fast and diving deep for fish.

Powerful front flippers

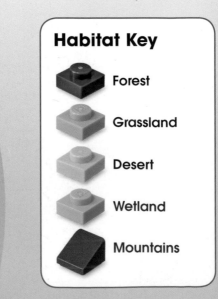

Where in the world?

SOUTH AMERICA

South America's most famous animal habitat is the Amazon rain forest, where a record-breaking variety of animals and plants live. But this continent also contains millions of miles of grassland, vast deserts, and islands that are home to some truly unique wildlife.

I'M SO GOOD AT HOLDING MY BREATH, I CAN EVEN SLEEP UNDERWATER!

Blue-footed booby

Tarantula

Giant anteater

Green turtle

Toucan

Giant tortoise

Guanaco

Andean condor

Sally Lightfoot crab

Tapir

Chinchilla

Habitat Key

Forest

Grassland

Desert

Wetland

Mountains

Sloth ▼

Sloths are seriously sleepy. They doze for more than 15 hours a day, hanging upside down in their favorite tree. Even when they're awake, they move so slowly that you might think they're still snoozing!

Lush, green rain forest

The giant Amazon river is surrounded by a warm, wet jungle of trees and plants. This kind of area is called rain forest, because it rains—a lot! The humid habitat is bursting with millions of different animals and plants, with new species being discovered every day.

Long, hooked claws for hanging off branches ......

Markings are good camouflage for lurking in muddy water .....

▲ Anaconda

This colossal crusher can weigh up to 550 lb (227 kg)—more than three adult men! It ambushes animals that come to drink at the river, trapping them in its coils.

Golden lion tamarin ▶

This monkey gets its name from the lion-like mane round its face. But, unlike the real thing, this lion lookalike is so tiny, it could sit on an adult human's hand.

Sensitive leg hairs detect prey

▲ Tarantula

Tarantulas are hairy spiders that live in burrows on the forest floor. Some grow as big as a dinner plate. At night, they hunt for insects, mice, and even birds.

Build it!

1x2 plate with ball

Balls and s-s-s-sockets

The anaconda's body is a chain of ball-and-socket plates. Its head is built around a plate with a ball.

MY BRIGHT COLORS SAY TO PREDATORS: "POISON—DO NOT EAT!"

Suction pads on toes help them cling to branches

Tree frog ▶

The warm, damp forest is an ideal home for tiny, brightly colored tree frogs. Some lay their eggs on leaves that overhang a pool. When the tadpoles hatch, they plop into the water below.

Rain forest trees form a thick layer of leaves called the canopy

Habitat facts

Scientists calculate that **10 percent** of all plants and animals live in the forests and rivers of the Amazon. That's truly amazing!

Rainforest plants give us many **favorite foods** such as coffee, chocolate, cashew nuts, avocados, and bananas.

Nose is 40 times more sensitive than a human's

I CAN SLURP UP MORE THAN 30,000 ANTS A DAY! YUM, YUM!

Anteater ▲

An anteater has a super-long snout and an even longer, sticky tongue. These are the ideal tools for its main activity—eating ants!

▲ Toucan

The toucan's bill is long, but it's also very light. This means the bird can perch on the thinnest branches and reach fruits that other birds can't get to.

Build it!

A nosey look

The anteater's long head is centered on two jumper plates. These attach sideways on an angle plate.

1x2x3 slope

1x2/2x2 angled plate

Jumper plate

High in the mountains

The Andes is a long chain of huge mountains that stretches down the continent of South America. Conditions can be desert-dry, hot and humid, or cold and windy. Andes animals have to be tough to survive life in the clouds.

▼ Chinchilla

The chinchilla's ultra-thick, soft fur keeps out the cold even on the highest mountaintop. Its gray color blends in with the rocks, helping it to hide from predators.

Bushy tail helps it to balance

▶ Guanaco

Guanacos and their descendants, llamas, are tough. They have to be, to survive where there's not much food or water and the air is thin and hard to breathe.

Woolly coat keeps out the cold

Small, spiky trees are well adapted to the harsh conditions

1x1 brick with four side studs

Build it!

Piggy in the middle

The guinea pig is hollow in the center! The sides are built separately and fit together using eight bricks with side studs.

Soft foot pads help to walk on rocky ground

◀ Guinea pig

Nobody knows how guinea pigs got their name—they don't come from Guinea and they're not pigs! These furry little rodents are the ancestors of the guinea pigs we keep as pets.

◄ Condor

These huge vultures use air currents that swirl above the mountains to help them fly. Condors can glide for more than an hour without flapping their wings.

Extra-long wings for sky-high soaring

Sharp eyes can spot prey far below

Rhea ►

In the rhea family, the male builds the nest, keeps the eggs safe, and looks after the young. The female still lays the eggs though—that's one job she can't get out of!

Rheas have wings but they can't fly

Habitat facts

In the shadow of the Andes is the Atacama desert, the driest place on the planet. Some parts have had **no rain in 400 years**!

The higher you go, the less oxygen there is in the air. Some animals have **extra red cells** in their blood, so it can carry more oxygen.

Hercules beetle ►

This brawny bug is long and very strong! It can carry more than 85 times its own weight. That's the same as a man lifting two elephants!

Body can be 7.5 in (19 cm) long

TAPIRS LIKE ME HAVE BEEN AROUND FOR 35 MILLION YEARS!

Thick, hairy coat

1x1 round plates with hole

Plate with side clip

Bar for proboscis

Build round a bar
The two sides of the beetle's shell attach to a central bar using plates with side clips. Another bar makes the insect's proboscis.

Build it!

Mountain tapir ▲

The tapir's bendy snout picks up grass to eat. It also acts as a snorkel when the tapir hides underwater from danger!

Three major **ocean currents** meet at the islands. The ancestors of today's animals rode these currents to reach their new home.

The Galápagos has a huge number of **unique animals**. About 97 percent of its reptiles are not found anywhere else in the world!

Isolated islands

Off the coast of South America are the remote, rocky Galápagos islands, the remains of mighty volcanoes that erupted 10 million years ago. The islands are now home to some of Earth's most weird and wonderful creatures.

BURP! WITHOUT ME, THE SHORE WOULD BE MUCH MESSIER!

▼ Sally Lightfoot crab

This crazy-colored crustacean is a vital member of the Galápagos clean-up crew. It eats virtually everything it finds on the shore, from seaweed to the remains of other crabs.

Nimble legs can scurry at top speed

▼ Green turtle

Sea turtles swim using their long, strong front flippers. They power gracefully through the water at up to 35 mph (50 kph).

Hard, protective shell

Scaly flippers

Make it snappy

The crab's claws are built with ball-and-socket joints, so they can move around. The pincers fit on to plates with rings.

Plate with socket

1x2 plate with ball

1x1 plate with ring

Build it!

Tooth and jaw
The iguana's jaw is an inverted slope piece. Its teeth are 1x1 round plates.

1x1 round plate

2x2 inverted slope

Build it!

▶ Marine iguana

Meet the only lizard that lives in the ocean. It spends its day diving underwater to nibble seaweed, then sunbathing on the rocks to warm up again.

⋯ **Flat tail for better swimming**

Extra-long claws to grip rocks ⋯

Frigatebird ▶

The male frigatebird is a huge show-off! To impress females, he blows up his chest, rattles his beak against it, and flaps his wings furiously.

Pouch of stretchy skin fills with air like a balloon ⋯

MY FEET ARE BLUER THAN YOURS!

MAYBE, BUT I HAVE THE SMOOTHEST DANCE MOVES, LOSER!

▼ Giant tortoise

The Galápagos tortoise is the largest on the planet, and can live for 150 years! It spends most of its time peacefully nibbling plants, fruit, and tree bark.

Body can be 4 ft (1.3 m) long

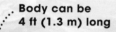

Webbed feet for swimming ⋯

Blue-footed booby ▲

The male booby does a slow, stomping dance to show off his blue feet. The ritual is to impress females and warn rival males off his territory.

I LOOK PRETTY GOOD FOR A HUNDRED-YEAR-OLD, DON'T I?

Long neck to reach high-up plants ⋮

29

AFRICA

The enormous continent of Africa is home to a brain-boggling variety of wildlife. From hot, dry deserts to steamy rain forests and vast, grassy plains, there's a perfect habitat on this continent for almost any animal you can think of!

1x2 brick with four side studs ...

Under the shell
This snail's shell is built around a brick with side studs. The top is made from two slope pieces.

Build it!

Giraffe

Addax

Fennec fox

Flamingo

Ring-tailed lemur

Giant land snail

Gorilla

Elephant

Lion

Warthog

Zebra

Camel

Habitat Key

- Forest
- Grassland
- Desert
- Scrubland
- Wetland
- Mountains

I'M THE SMALLEST FOX IN THE WORLD, WITH THE BIGGEST EARS!

Record breakers

The world's **biggest land animal** is the African elephant. It can weigh more than 80 adult humans together!

Africa is the only place where **gorillas**, **giraffes**, **zebras**, and **hippos** live in the wild.

LEMURS LIKE ME ONLY LIVE HERE IN MADAGASCAR!

Dry, dusty deserts

MY EGGS ARE SO BIG, IT WOULD TAKE AN HOUR TO HARD-BOIL ONE!

The Sahara desert stretches over about one-quarter of Africa. During the day, it's one of the hottest places on Earth, but at night, the temperature dips dramatically. It hardly ever rains, and fierce winds blow up sudden, blinding sandstorms. No animals could live in such an extreme place, right? Wrong!

Strong, muscly legs

▲ Ostrich

Never try to race an ostrich! It's the fastest two-legged animal on Earth, and can reach speeds of 45 mph (70 kph)!

I CAN HEAR MICE SCURRY ON THE SAND HUNDREDS OF YARDS AWAY!

Fennec fox ▶

The supersized ears of a Fennec fox pick up the sounds of prey. They also help to keep the fox cool by giving off heat, like mini-radiators.

Furry footpads protect paws from hot sand

Armor-plated body

Bendy tail delivers sting

Scorpion ▲

The scorpion's secret weapon is in its tail. It grabs prey in its huge front claws, then arches its tail over to inject a dose of paralyzing poison into them.

Plate with ring of bars

Build it!

Arms for legs

The scorpion's legs are skeleton arm pieces. They clip onto a plate with a ring of bars, just like the head and tail.

Skeleton arm

Plate with top clip

Addax add-ons

The addax's horns are made from LEGO® NINJAGO® blade pieces. Each one fits onto a plate with a top clip, and can be tilted to any angle.

Build it!

▼ Desert locust

Most of the time, these members of the grasshopper family are harmless. But sometimes, they collect in a huge, hungry swarm. A greedy gang can gobble up a whole field of grass in a few minutes!

Long, spiral-shaped horns

Powerful back legs

► Addax

Like many desert animals, the addax doesn't need to drink. It gets the water it needs from the grass it grazes on.

Habitat facts

Giant Sahara sand dunes can be **1,500 ft (450 m) tall**. That's so high that you could completely bury France's Eiffel Tower inside one dune!

The desert gets busier when night falls. This is because many animals rest through the **heat of the day** and come out when it's cooler.

Double row of eyelashes keeps out sand

Fat stored in the hump provides energy when there's no food

ONE HUMP OR TWO?

Camel ►

Camels are built for desert survival and can go for days without drinking. African camels have a single hump on their back, while their Asian cousins have two.

Knee pads for kneeling down

33

Where in Africa?

African grassy plains

The grassy plains of Africa are called the savanna. For half of the year it's hot and dry, and survival is a daily struggle for wildlife. Then, when the rains finally come, many animals feast on the seas of lush, green grass that spring up almost overnight.

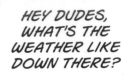

HEY DUDES, WHAT'S THE WEATHER LIKE DOWN THERE?

◀ Giraffe

Meet the tallest of Earth's animals! The giraffe's long neck means it can reach juicy leaves in the highest treetops.

Male lions have a shaggy mane

Lion ▶

Lions live in a family group called a pride, with the strongest male in charge. He protects the pride, while the females hunt together to find food for everyone.

MY ROAR IS SO LOUD THAT YOU CAN HEAR IT 5 MILES AWAY!

▼ Warthog

The warthog can use its tusks to defend itself. But this peace-loving wild pig prefers to use them to dig up tasty roots from the savanna soil.

Build it!

1x2 jumper plate

1x1 plate with top clip

Back end of a warthog

Build sideways from the back of the warthog to attach the tail. Use a jumper plate to center it.

▼ Rhinoceros

The rhino's main interest is munching grass. But with its massive body and huge, pointed horn, it can launch a fierce attack if it feels threatened.

Tough, leathery skin

I CAN RUN AS FAST AS AN OLYMPIC SPRINTER!

Build it!

From ear to ear
Each of the elephant's ears fits onto a plate with an angled bar. This means they can flap, just like in real life!

1x2 plate with bar

.1x1 plate with top clip

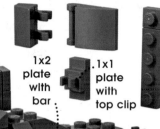

▼ Zebra

Nobody knows for sure why zebras have stripes. But no two zebras look exactly the same—each has its own unique pattern.

Tusks are made of ivory

Strong legs to run away from danger

Elephant ▶

African elephants are huge, with an appetite to match! They can eat up to 550 lb (250 kg) of grass and leaves in a day.

Trunk sucks in water and picks up food

I'M CALLED A CROWNED CRANE BECAUSE OF MY COOL CREST OF FEATHERS!

◀ Crane

This bird's long neck and good eyesight help it spot danger as it hides in long grass.

Habitat facts

The baobab tree is able to **survive the dry season** because it can store up to 32,000 gallons (120,000 litres) of water in its trunk.

Grass fires are common in the savanna. They make the **soil more fertile** and also create space for new plants to grow.

35

Rivers and jungles

The Congo Basin is a vast area of forests, lakes, and swamps around the Congo River. It's bigger than the whole of Europe, and its forests are so thick that some parts have never been explored by humans!

▼ Giant land snail

The largest snail on the planet has a shell as big as a baseball and a huge appetite to match. It will munch on almost any plant it finds, from dead leaves to bananas.

···· Stripy shell

Eyes on stalks ····

UNDER THIS SHELL, I'M A TOTAL SOFTY. I HAVE NO BONES AT ALL!

▼ Hippopotamus

Hippos spend the daytime wallowing in lakes and rivers, to keep out of the scorching sun. At dusk, they come onto land to graze on grass and plants.

IT'S ALMOST DINNER TIME —HIPPO, HIPPO HURRAY!

Beak scoops up shrimp from the water

I SHARE A LAKE WITH MY FLAMINGO FRIENDS—MORE THAN A MILLION OF THEM!

◄ Flamingo

Flamingoes are not pink when they hatch. They get their color from the shrimp and other tiny water creatures that they eat.

Long legs for wading in lakes

Skin dries out if it gets too much sun

Hungry hippo

A pair of 1x2 plates with clips are built into the hippo's back to make a sturdy connection for its gaping mouth.

···· 1x2 plate with bar

1x2 plate with clip ····

Build it!

Chimpanzee ▶

The clever chimp uses things around it as tools. A stick can dig out tasty insects, and a rock makes a handy nutcracker.

Build it!

Creature feature

The chameleon's curly tongue is a minifigure lasso on a jumper plate.

.. Lasso

1x2 jumper plate

Spotted coat for camouflage

Long, sticky tongue to catch insects .....

> **HEY, WHAT'S GOING ON? THAT CHAMELEON WAS BROWN A MINUTE AGO!**

▲ Leopard

If you want to spot a leopard, look up! Leopards love climbing trees. A tall branch is the perfect place to eat a meal in peace, look out for danger, or just have a cat nap!

Chameleon ▲

These extraordinary lizards can change their skin color according to their mood. Also, their eyes swivel separately to look in two directions at once!

Curly tail wraps around branches

> **I'M A TYPE OF MAMMAL CALLED A PRIMATE—AND SO ARE YOU, HUMAN!**

Habitat facts

The Congo forest is **dreadfully dark**! In some parts, the trees are so thick that only 1 percent of sunlight reaches the forest floor.

The Congo River, which flows through the rain forest, is the **deepest river** in the world. More than 700 types of fish live in it.

◀ Gorilla

This heavyweight hulk can weigh as much as four humans! But gorillas live a mostly quiet life, hanging out with their family, snoozing, or nibbling leaves in the forest.

.... Gorillas usually walk on all four legs

37

Iceland is also part of Europe, but it's too far north to appear on this map.

EUROPE

Many parts of Europe are crowded with people, but there's still room for an awesome array of wildlife. A lot of forest that once covered the continent has been replaced by farmland and towns, but many animals have adapted well to their new habitats.

Habitat Key

Forest

Desert

Woodland

Scrubland

Grassland

Ice

Build it!

The studs that make a squirrel

The details that make this squirrel are built around a brick with two side studs and a headlight brick.

1x1 brick with two side studs

Headlight brick

TIME TO TAKE A NAP. WAKE ME UP IN SIX MONTHS!

I CAN EAT 200 EARTHWORMS IN ONE NIGHT. BET YOU CAN'T!

A MOTHER RABBIT LIKE ME CAN HAVE 100 BABIES A YEAR. THAT'S A LOT OF BUNNIES!

Record breakers

The wolf is the **largest member** of the dog family. Wolves once roamed all over Europe, but now live mainly in remote forests in the north.

Reindeer are the only **type of deer** where both the males and females grow antlers!

Red fox	**Red squirrel**	**Brown bear**	**Barn owl**

Otter	**Badger**	**Mole**	**Hedgehog**

Rabbit	**Wolf**	**Reindeer**	**Bumble bee**

Cool forests of the north

Enormous forests, called taiga, stretch across Europe's northern zone. Summers are short and winters are long and snowy. Animals have to be tough to survive months of freezing weather and not much food.

Brown bear ▲

Brown bears sleep through winter, when food is hard to find. They eat as much as they can beforehand, to store energy in their bodies to keep them going while they snooze.

Shaggy fur keeps out the cold

▼ Whooper swan

Swans are very romantic! When a male and female pair up, they stay together their whole lives, producing babies (called cygnets) every spring.

Beaver ▼

Beavers are brilliant builders. They cut down trees with their strong teeth to make a dam across a stream. Then they build a cozy den, called a lodge, in the pond made by the dam.

I LOVE GNAWING AND BUILDING, WHICH IS LUCKY BECAUSE IT'S PRETTY MUCH ALL I DO!

Flat tail for steering in water

Long, bendy neck

Warm, waterproof fur

Build it!

Brick your neck out

The swan's elegant neck flexes on hinges made from clips and bars. Its head is a brick with four side studs.

1x1 plate with top clip

1x2 plate with end bar

1x1 plate with clip

JUST REMEMBER, I'M TOP DOG AROUND HERE!

Wolves have excellent night vision

1x2 curved half arch

Build it!

Linking up the lynx
Build the lynx's legs last, using small curved half arches. Then lock them onto its body with 1x3 plates.

◀ Wolf
Wolves live in family groups, with the strongest male in charge. They hunt as a team, which means they can take on large animals like reindeer.

Long legs for chasing prey

I LOOK CUTE, BUT DON'T BE FOOLED—I'M FUR-OCIOUS!

Large, fuzz-covered antlers

Double-thick, woolly coat

Hairy paws for walking on snow

▲ Lynx
The lynx is one of the forest's most cunning hunters. This fearless feline takes on reindeer more than three times its size!

Nose can sniff out food even under snow

▲ Reindeer
In summer, these large deer munch the grass and new trees that spring up when the warmer weather arrives. In the winter, they use their hooves and snouts to dig out mosses growing under the snow.

Habitat facts

Taiga forest is mainly made of **tough conifer trees**, such as pine and spruce. Their needle-shaped, frostproof leaves are smooth so snow slides off them easily.

The forest is much less busy in winter. Many birds fly to **warmer places**, while animals, such as snakes and bats, sleep through the coldest months.

Woodland wildlife

Shh! Next time you visit the woods you might, if you're quiet, see all kinds of animals, from a scurrying mouse to a silent, swooping owl. Woodland trees make perfect homes for many different creatures, providing food, shelter, and hiding places.

I'M GOING TO THE POND FOR MY MORNING MOSQUITO SNACK!

····· Eyes can see in
all directions

▲ Dragonfly

Dragonflies are expert fliers. They can zoom forwards and backwards or up and down, and even hover like a helicopter. They can catch and eat insects in mid-air, too!

Habitat facts

Food can be hard to find in the winter, so some animals just **snooze until spring**! This long, deep sleep is called hibernation.

An oak tree makes a great **bug hotel.** Just one tree can be home to 350 different species of insect.

Streamlined body
helps it swim fast

Otter ▶

Baby otters are called pups. Their games and play-fights help them learn the skills they need to become efficient underwater hunters.

Webbed feet ······

Badgers have
a super sense
of smell

I'M NOCTURNAL, SO I SLEEP ALL DAY AND HUNT AT NIGHT!

◀ Badger

The badger uses its strong claws to dig in the earth for worms and insects. It lives in a big burrow made of tunnels and chambers, called a sett.

Wings are made of stretchy skin

Strong claws for hanging upside down

▲ Bat

Bats find prey by making squeaking and clicking noises. The sounds echo off passing insects and help the bat to pinpoint their location.

▼ Rabbit

The best time to spot a rabbit is very early in the morning, or just before dark. When they're not out looking for tasty plants to nibble, rabbits live in underground burrows called warrens.

Long ears pick up sounds of danger

Large front teeth for gnawing

THAT OWL HAS HIS EYE ON ME. I'D BETTER HOP AWAY!

Long, strong back legs

NOT ALL OWLS HOOT, YOU KNOW. I PREFER TO SCREECH!

Hooked beak

Strong, sharp talons

◄ Barn owl

Three secret weapons make the barn owl an expert night hunter: sharp eyesight, sensitive hearing, and feathers soft enough to swoop down silently on prey.

Build it!

Bushy tail

Turning tail

A 1x1 plate with a bar at the base of the squirrel's tail allows the tail to move from side to side and up and down.

1x2 plate with clip

1x2 plate with bar

...1x1 plate with bar

Red squirrel ►

In the fall, squirrels collect nuts and bury them in the ground. In the winter, when food is scarce, they dig up the nuts—if they can remember where they put them!

Urban animals

You might think a big, busy city like London, England is the last place to find wildlife. But if an animal can cope with the hustle and bustle, a city can actually be an ideal home, providing plenty of food, shelter, and warmth.

Ultra-fast fluttering wings make a buzzing noise

MY BLACK AND YELLOW STRIPES WARN ENEMIES TO BUZZ OFF!

▲ Bumble bee

Bumble bees busily fly round city parks and gardens, drinking sweet nectar from flowers. One bee might visit 200,000 flowers in its lifetime!

I SWALLOW FISH HEAD FIRST, SO THEIR SCALES DON'T STICK IN MY THROAT!

Pointed beak for spearing fish

Kingfisher ▶

The bright blue kingfisher has become more common along city rivers and canals. This is partly because the water is cleaner now, so there are more fish for the kingfisher to hunt.

Waterproof feathers

I'M A MALE MALLARD. I'M MUCH MORE COLORFUL THAN MY FEMALE MATE!

▲ Mallard

As long as there's a pond or stream nearby, ducks can live very well in cities. In fact, ducks live in every part of the world, except Antarctica.

Build it!

1x1 brick with four side studs

Duck build

This mallard's bill, eyes, and head plumage are built around a brick with side studs, centered on a jumper plate.

1x2 jumper plate

2x2 jumper plate

▼ Red fox

Foxes will eat lots of different foods, from mice and birds to berries and insects. City foxes also enjoy tasty take-out meals by raiding garbage cans for the food that we throw away.

A fox can hear a mouse 33 ft (100 m) away, even if it's underground!

Habitat facts

Peregrine falcons usually hunt from clifftops. But city peregrines **nest on skyscrapers** instead, diving off them and swooping down on birds flying below.

Gardens are home to an **amazing variety** of wildlife! A city garden can contain hundreds of species of insects, spiders, and worms.

CITY FOXES LIKE ME MAKE OUR DENS UNDER GARDEN SHEDS.

Turn that snout about
The rat's snout is built sideways and fitted to a brick with one side stud.

1x1 brick with one side stud

1x1 brick with two side studs

Build it!

Rat ▶

The rat is a survival expert—it can live almost anywhere. It's a great climber, jumper, digger, and swimmer. In fact, if rats were human, they'd be Olympic champions!

Long whiskers help to find the way in the dark

▼ Mole

You might never spot a mole, but little piles of earth on the lawn are sure signs that a mole has been hard at work digging tunnels under your garden!

Sharp spikes keep nosy predators away

Snuffly nose sniffs out prey

MY LUXURY BURROW HAS MANY ROOMS. THERE'S EVEN ONE FOR STORING WORMS!

▲ Hedgehog

City people like to see hedgehogs in their gardens. They know that a hedgehog means a lot fewer snails and slugs to munch on their flowers and vegetables!

Strong front feet for digging

45

ASIA

More than half of the people on the planet live in Asia. It's Earth's largest continent, so there's plenty of space left for animals, too. Amazing Asia contains both the highest and the lowest habitats on Earth— the Himalayan mountains and the Dead Sea.

WHICH BIRD HAS THE LONGEST FEATHERS? YOU GUESSED— IT'S ME!

Panda

Yak

Water buffalo

Peacock

Snow leopard

Red panda

Orangutan

Tiger

Birdwing butterfly

Slow loris

King cobra

Komodo dragon

Record breakers

The 10 **highest mountains** are all in Asia. The highest peak, Mount Everest, is 29,029 ft (8,848 m) above sea level—and it's growing by 0.2 in (5 mm) every year!

The Siberian tiger is the **world's largest big cat**. Experts believe there are only about 500 left in the wild.

I'M A WILD YAK. I DON'T DO CHORES LIKE MY DOMESTICATED COUSINS!

I'M A SLOW LORIS. THE CLUE'S IN THE NAME— HURRYING IS SO NOT MY THING!

Habitat Key

- Rainforest
- Woodland
- Grassland
- Desert
- Scrubland
- Water
- Wetland
- Mountains

Build it!

Branches make the ape

Almost all of this orangutan is built sideways, branching off a central brick with side studs.

Sideways headlight brick

1x1 brick with four side studs

47

Birdwing butterfly ▼

This awe-inspring insect has a wingspan as wide as an adult's hand! It feeds on nectar from flowers that grow high up among the rain forest trees.

· Wings are shaped like birds' wings

Tropical island animals

Islands are often home to animals that don't live anywhere else. Many of the islands that make up Indonesia have a similar forest habitat, but the animals on different islands have evolved in lots of different ways.

◄ Flying squirrel

These furry tree-dwellers can't fly like birds, but they do glide long distances as they leap from tree to tree.

· Flaps of skin act like a parachute

Komodo dragon ▶

This marauding monster is the planet's largest lizard. It's heavier than a man, and can knock down a deer with a flick of its tail.

I CAN'T BREATHE FIRE LIKE STORYBOOK DRAGONS, BUT I DO SPIT POISON!

Build it!

1x2 plate with three bars

Get to grips with claws

The lizard's feet are equipped with adjustable claws. They splay out from a plate with three bars.

Plate with top clip

1x1 round plate with hole

.... Horn piece

... Sharp claws for tearing meat

▼ Orangutan

Orangutans spend almost all their time high in the treetops. Every night, they build a new leafy nest to sleep in among the branches.

Ultra-long arms are perfect for swinging from branches

Habitat facts

Borneo's rain forest is **140 million years old**, making it one of Earth's oldest. The island's Indonesian name is "Kalimantan," meaning "burning-weather island."

The huge Titan arum plant from Sumatra is also called the **corpse flower**, because it produces a bloom that gives off a smell like rotting meat!

MY NAME MEANS "PERSON OF THE FOREST" IN THE MALAY LANGUAGE!

Slow loris ▶

A mother slow loris smears her baby's fur with toxic goo from a gland on her arm. Predators get a nasty shock if they try to take a bite of baby!

Long-fingered hands can grip thin branches

Hands can grip things as well as human hands can

The huge *Rafflesia* flower grows to 3 ft 3 in (1 m) in diameter

Hook-like feet for clinging to twigs

▲ Giant stick insect

The world's longest insect can grow to twice the height of this book! Staying still and looking like a twig is its brilliant tactic to keep safe from predators.

Shady groves of bamboo

Amid the cold, snowy slopes of the Himalayan mountains lie thick, green forests of bamboo. This tall, fast-growing grass is utterly irresistible to one of the planet's most famous animals—the giant panda.

Habitat facts

The Himalayas are the world's **highest mountains**. The word "himalaya" means "home of snow" in the Sanskrit language.

Bamboo is the **fastest-growing plant** in the world. A tropical bamboo can grow an amazing 3 ft 3 in (1 m) in one day!

▼ Golden pheasant

Male golden pheasants are colorful, but females are pale brown. Their dull coloring helps to keep them safer from predators while they care for their chicks.

The male's neck feathers rise to make a colorful collar

Extra-long tail feathers

Tufted deer ▶

A male tufted deer has a special weapon it uses on other males that come too close—a pair of miniature, spiky tusks!

Long, curved horns

◀ Yak

The shaggy-haired yak has two layers of fur to help it survive in the snowy mountains. The waterproof top layer is lined with fleecy fur to keep the heat in.

Big hooves for walking on snow

YAKS LOVE CHILLING! IN THE SUMMER, WE MOVE TO COLDER PLACES.

Look into the eyes

All the animals on these pages have eyes made from printed 1x1 round tiles attached to headlight bricks.

Headlight brick ...

Printed eye tile

Build it!

◀ Snow leopard

These beautiful big cats are so well camouflaged and stealthy that you could be right next to one and still not notice it. No wonder local people call it the mountain ghost!

.... **The leopard wraps its tail around itself to keep warm at night**

OH DEER, I CAN'T KEEP UP... NO SUPPER FOR ME TONIGHT!

Red panda ▼

The red panda spends most of its time in the trees. It climbs to the highest branches to snooze, sunbathe, or stay clear of predators.

Huge paws tipped with sharp claws

Thick, red-brown or chestnut fur

Hands are good at gripping bamboo

I'M SO COOL! I CAN LIVE IN COLDER PLACES THAN ANY OTHER MONKEY.

Super-short nose

▲ Giant panda

The shy, secretive panda lives in remote mountain forests. Pandas have two main activities: sleeping and eating bamboo. They spend almost all their time doing one or the other!

◀ Snub-nose monkey

With its little blue face, this monkey looks as if it has frostbite! But its silky fur keeps it warm in the freezing mountain winters.

51

Monsoon forests

Parts of India are covered in forests where it's dry for most of the year—then lots of rain falls in one short, soggy season. The dry season is tough for animals because food is scarce. It's also harder to hide from danger because the trees are bare.

▼ King cobra

This formidable hunter mainly preys on other snakes. It injects victims with deadly venom via its long, needle-shaped fangs.

AT 18 FT (15.5 M) LONG, I'M THE WORLD'S LONGEST VENOMOUS SNAKE!

The cobra flattens out its neck to look even bigger and fiercer

Feathers have spots called eyes

PHEW! IT'S HARD WORK CONVINCING FEMALES I'M GORGEOUS!

Peacock ▶

Male peacocks are big show-offs! They fan out and shake their spectacular tail feathers to try to attract females.

Brown, black, or red fur

▲ Giant squirrel

The tail of this supersized squirrel is longer than its head and body together! The trailing tail helps the squirrel to balance on its back legs as it snacks on berries or fruit.

Build it!

Your biggest fan

Make a fantail for your peacock using 1x1 round plates on curved plates. Then attach the fan at an angle using a hinge brick.

Hinge brick

▼ Hornbill

Hornbills feed mainly on fruit they like figs best. Hornbills help new trees to grow by scattering fruit seeds across the forest floor in their droppings!

Huge beak top is called a casque

Stripy coat blends with tall grass

Tiger ▶

The tiger is the largest of the big cats and an awesomely powerful hunter. Unlike most cats, tigers like water. Some even jump into lakes to hunt crocodiles!

I CAN LEAP UP TO 20 FT (6 M), SO DON'T BOTHER CLIMBING A TREE TO ESCAPE ME!

Long, sharp canine teeth for gripping prey

▼ Water buffalo

When the heat is on, the water buffalo takes time out in a muddy water hole. This keeps the buffalo cool and protects it from bothersome biting insects.

Horns are among the longest in the animal kingdom

MY HUMUNGOUS HORNS SHOULD CONVINCE THAT TIGER TO STEER CLEAR!

Habitat facts

In the dry season, food in the forest is hard to find. Many plants have **thorns or spikes**, which stops hungry creatures from nibbling them.

The rainy season is short but very wet! Some areas get 11 ft (3.5 m) of rain, falling in **heavy downpours** every day for four months.

Build it!

Pin the tail on the buffalo

The buffalo's tail is a curved slope piece. It attaches sideways to a LEGO® Technic half pin in a brick with a hole.

1x2 LEGO Technic brick with hole

LEGO Technic half pin

WE DOLPHINS LIKE HUMANS—YOU'RE ALMOST AS INTELLIGENT AS US!

AUSTRALASIA

Australasia is made up of Australia, which is the world's largest island, and thousands of smaller islands, scattered in the Pacific ocean. This remote continent is full of curious creatures that can't be found anywhere else.

Kangaroo

Bird of paradise

Kiwi

Duck-billed platypus

Blue-ringed octopus

Koala

Jellyfish

Bottlenose dolphin

Clownfish

Starfish

Habitat Key

Forest

Desert

Woodland

Scrubland

Grassland

Mountains

FEMALES FLOCK TO ME WHEN I FLASH MY FABULOUS FEATHERS!

Build it!

Super star
Five hinge plates overlap to make this simple but clever starfish. Each leg is made with two hinges and a 1x2 plate.

····· 1x2 plate

Hinge plate ·····

Record breakers

There are only five kinds of mammal that **lay eggs** instead of having live babies—and all of them live in Australasia.

The blue-ringed jellyfish is only the size of a golf ball, but it contains **enough venom** to kill 26 humans in minutes!

WHAT HAS A BEAVER'S TAIL, AN OTTER'S BODY AND A DUCK'S BILL? ME, OBVIOUSLY!

I HAVE BLUE BLOOD AND THREE HEARTS. HOW COOL AM I?

55

I'M SO FAST, ONLY A CROCODILE CAN CATCH ME! UH-OH, IS THAT WHAT I THINK IT IS?

Animals down under

In Australia, almost 90 percent of people live on the coast, where the weather is pleasant and there is plenty of water. The vast, remote center is called the Outback. Most of it is dry, dusty, and sizzling hot. In spite of the harsh conditions, many animals have adapted well.

Pointed beak for pecking at berries, fruit, and seeds

Feathers look like shaggy hair

▲ Emu

With their small, weak wings and bulky bodies, emus can't fly. They are superb runners and swimmers though, so don't challenge one to a race!

Duck-billed platypus ▼

The platypus lives in a riverbank burrow. It hunts for food along the muddy riverbed, using its big, rubbery snout to feel for food in the murky water.

Flat tail helps to steer underwater

Legging it

Six of this spider's legs fit onto a plate with a ring of bars. The other two attach to a plate with three bars—as do the eyes above.

Build it!

Plate with side clip

1x2 plate with three bars

Plate with ring of bars

Webbed feet for swift swimming

◀ Redback spider

Watch out for the female redback! She may be tiny, but her powerful fangs can bite through human skin and inject dangerous venom.

Long legs are covered in hairs that sense movement

▼ Kangaroo

Kangaroos don't walk or run—they jump! Their powerful back legs move them forward in huge leaps, while their heavy tails help them to balance as they bounce along.

Short front legs are mostly used for grasping food

► Saltwater crocodile

This scary, scaly snapper is the biggest, baddest reptile in the world. It's powerful enough to seize and devour any mammals it comes across—including humans!

Eyes on top of head allow it to see when its body is underwater

I'M JUST GOING TO GRAB A QUICK SNACK...

Build it!

Not just a pretty face

The koala's head is a clever combination of hinge plates for sideways building in two directions.

1x2½ angled plate

1x2/2x2 angled plate

◄ Koala

Koalas are the pickiest eaters ever! They only eat the leaves of a few types of eucalyptus tree. And even then, they just pick the tastiest leaves and reject the others.

IS IT BEDTIME YET? I NEED MY 20 HOURS A DAY TO STAY IN PEAK CONDITION!

Sharp claws for gripping trees

57

Colorful coral reefs

▼ Bottlenose dolphin

Dolphins can leap out the water high enough to jump over a double-decker bus! They communicate by making different clicking and whistling noises.

Long, streamlined body

Under the warm, shallow waters off the coast of Australia is a colourful habitat—the Great Barrier Reef. Looking like an underwater mountain range, the reef is made from corals. Coral seems like rock but is actually formed by tiny animals, which have a hard outer shell of limestone.

OK, I'M NOT ACTUALLY A FISH, BUT TO MY FANS, I'M A BIG STAR!

A sensor at the end of each arm can tell the difference between light and dark ...

Underneath are hundreds of tiny, tube-shaped feet

◀ Starfish

If a starfish loses an arm, it has the amazing ability to grow a new one. First, a tiny bud appears. In just a few months, the bud grows into a full-sized replacement.

Paddle-shaped tail for fast swimming

1x1 round plate

Hinge plate

Build it!

Underneath the stars

The five segments of the starfish are connected with hinge plates. Add 1x1 round plates to make realistic suckers.

▲ Sea krait

This stripy snake hunts among the corals for small fish, which it kills with a deadly bite from its venomous fangs.

Reef shark ▶

A coral reef is like an all-you-can-eat buffet for the reef shark. After dark, it patrols rocky crevices, on the lookout for fish, crabs, and squid.

Pointed snout is excellent at sensing prey

BELIEVE ME, I'D MUCH RATHER HIDE UNDER A ROCK THAN ATTACK YOU!

1x1 angled tooth plate

A build with bite

The roof of the shark's mouth is made with six angled tooth plates. Its lower jaw has three sideways 1x2 tooth plates.

1x2 tooth plate

Build it!

Tentacles are used to sense surroundings

◀ Blue-ringed octopus

Sometimes, the smallest creatures can be the deadliest. A single venomous sting from this mini-monster could kill a human in less than an hour.

Clownfish ▶

The clownfish keeps safe by hiding among a sea anemone's tentacles. In return, it keeps the anemone clean and chases away other fish.

Body opens and closes to move through the water

▲ Purple stinger jellyfish

When it comes to animals, the jellyfish is a basic model! It has no brain, heart, or bones—it's really just a squishy body with a mouth, a stomach, and some long tentacles to catch food.

Habitat facts

The reef contains a huge **range of creatures**—more than 1,500 kinds of fish, 30 species of whales and dolphins, and 5,000 mollusks.

The Great Barrier Reef is so big, it can be **seen from space**. It's 1,250 miles (2,000 km) long and covers the same area as Italy!

59

THE ARCTIC

Record breakers

The Greenland shark can live for 400 years, but another Arctic animal can **live even longer**. A clam caught in 2006 was found to be 508 years old!

IF IT GETS ABOVE FREEZING, I CALL THAT A HEATWAVE!

I'M STANDING ON TOP OF THE WORLD!

The Arctic region is made up of the most northern parts of the continents of Europe, Asia, and North America, and the sea around them.

Polar bear

Harp seal

Musk ox

Arctic fox

Walrus

The Arctic and Antarctica are areas at the far north and south of our planet. These places are extremely cold, and for half the year they get almost no sunlight. Survival is a struggle, but lots of tough animals are up to the challenge!

Antarctica is a triple record breaker—it's the **coldest**, **windiest**, and **driest** place on the planet. Brr!

Giant squid

Albatross

Emperor penguin and chick

Orca

Elephant seal

Skua

Unlike the Arctic, Antarctica is a continent in its own right.

I'M THE LARGEST MEMBER OF THE DOLPHIN FAMILY!

I LIVE SO DEEP IN THE OCEAN THAT HARDLY ANY HUMANS HAVE SEEN ME!

Where in the world?

Habitat key

Forest

Water

Snow

Ice

Mountains

ANTARCTICA

Seas of ice

The North Pole is the most northerly point on Earth

▼ Arctic fox

Like many animals who live here, the Arctic fox can change color. Its coat is brown during the summer, but in the winter, its fur turns snowy white.

Coat grows extra thick in winter

The Arctic is the most northern area on Earth. It's mostly made of ocean, with a vast sheet of ice floating in it. The Arctic has two seasons: summer and winter—but even the warmest months stay pretty chilly. Arctic plants and animals need to withstand bitter cold, ice, and snow.

I LOVE CLAMS SO MUCH THAT I CAN GOBBLE UP 4,000 OF THEM IN ONE MEAL!

Long tusks help to pull the body out of the water

▼ Harp seal

Harp seals have their babies on newly formed ice. It's thick enough for the seals to live on, but much too thin to support any polar bears that might come to prey on the pups.

MY PUP BLENDS SO WELL WITH THE SNOW THAT EVEN I CAN'T SPOT HIM!

▲ Walrus

On land, the walrus is slow and clumsy. But in water, it's a swift, sleek swimmer, using its huge flippers to power through the ocean.

Thick layer of blubber keeps seals warm

Build it!

1x2 friction ball plate

1x2 friction socket plate

Flexible flippers

Ball-and-socket friction joints make these seals' flippers just as flexible as the real thing!

◄ Musk ox

Musk oxen stay safe from predators by living together in herds. If they are threatened, they huddle in a circle, with their sharp horns pointing outward.

Wide hooves dig under the snow for plants ......

Beak can hold up to 60 fish at a time ......

Puffin ►

With its big, colorful, stripy beak, bright orange feet, and loud squawk, the puffin is one Arctic resident that's definitely not trying to blend in!

Habitat facts

The Arctic ocean is rich in plant-like algae and tiny creatures. So for animals that can adapt to the cold, there's **plenty of food** in this deep freeze!

Only a few bird species stay in the Arctic all year. When winter arrives, **many birds migrate** to warmer places to find food.

◄ Polar bear

The polar bear is the world's biggest bear, and a truly awesome predator. Its main prey is the seal, but a hungry bear will try to catch virtually any creature it comes across —even a human!

SOMETIMES I'LL WAIT ALL DAY FOR A SEAL TO POP UP, THEN TWO COME ALONG AT ONCE!

Huge claws grip the ice .....

Build it!

1x2 friction ball plate ...

Polar poser

The polar bear's legs can be posed in different ways thanks to several ball-and-socket friction joints.

1x1 angled tooth plate ...

1x2 friction socket plate .....

1x2 ball-and-socket plate

The South Pole is the most southerly point on Earth

Southern snowy deserts

Antarctica is a huge, frozen continent surrounded by sea that's mostly ice, too. It's too cold and dry for most plants, so nearly all Antarctic animals get their food from the sea. The only land animals who can live here all year are seals and penguins.

▼ Elephant seal

When it is hunting for fish, the elephant seal dives down more than half a mile (1 km). It can hold its breath for a lung-busting two hours!

MALES LIKE ME CAN WEIGH AS MUCH AS 27 ADULT HUMANS!

Nose looks like an elephant's trunk

Eyes as big as soccer balls

I CAN GROW TO 66 FT (20M) LONG —THAT'S LONGER THAN A BUS!

Two long tentacles grab prey

Eight arms hold prey while the squid eats it

Brick with hole

Tackle a tentacle

Plug long tail pieces into bricks with holes to make the squid's long tentacles. Slot tooth parts into elephant's trunk pieces at the other end.

Long tail piece

Elephant's trunk

Tooth piece

Build it!

◀ Giant squid

This deep-sea monster is seriously secretive! It took until the year 2007 for humans to capture a live giant squid.

Albatross ▼

With its super-long, slim wings, the albatross can stay in the air for days. It soars over the ocean, spotting fish and squid that pop up to the surface.

Hooked bill

HEY! LEAVE SOME FISH FOR ME, YOU GREEDY OLD ORCA!

Habitat facts

If you hate bugs, move to Antarctica! Only **one insect** lives there—the tiny Antarctic midge.

Antarctica's land is permanently covered by a **layer of ice** that's a mile (1.6 km) thick.

Build it!

Plate with end bar

1x1 slope

1x1 plate with top clip

A fin to finish
The orca's fin is angled on a hinge made from a plate with a bar and a plate with a clip.

Powerful tail drives its body through the water

I'M THE BIGGEST PENGUIN. THAT'S WHY THEY CALL ME AN EMPEROR!

▲ Orca

The orca is sometimes called the wolf of the sea, as it's such a fast and fierce predator. Orcas live in family groups that eat, sleep, play, and hunt together.

Sharp beak to spear fish and shrimp

HEY, PENGUIN DADDY! WANT TO TRY MY NEW PENGUIN BABY-SITTING SERVICE?

◄ Antarctic skua

This polar pirate has a habit of stealing penguins' eggs to eat. It even snatches baby penguins if it gets the chance!

Broad, strong wings

◄ Emperor penguin

Emperor penguins take turns as parents. While one swims off in search of food, the other stays on the ice to protect their chick.

65

GLOSSARY

Adaptation
The way an animal changes to become better suited to its habitat. For instance, moles have adapted to living underground.

Algae
Simple plants that grow in water. Seaweeds are a type of algae.

Ancestor
An animal from the past that another more recent animal is related to.

Antennae
A pair of long, thin feelers on the head, which some animals, especially insects, use to smell, touch, or hear.

Bill
Another word for a bird's beak.

Bird
One of a group of animals that have wings, feathers, and a beak. Most birds can fly. Puffins are birds.

Burrow
A hole or tunnel underground where an animal lives. A rabbit lives in a burrow.

Camouflage
A color or pattern that blends in with an animal's surroundings, helping to disguise it.

Canine tooth
A pointed tooth used to grasp and tear food. Carnivores often have long, sharp canines.

Carnivore
An animal that eats meat. Polar bears are carnivores.

Conifer
A type of tree that has needle-like leaves, which it keeps all year round.

Climate
The normal weather you can expect in an area over a period of time.

Continent
A huge area of land. There are seven continents on Earth: Africa, Antarctica, Asia, Australasia, Europe, North America, and South America.

Crustacean
An animal that has a hard outer shell and two pairs of antennae. Crabs are crustaceans.

Descendant
An animal that is related to another type of animal that lived before it.

Domesticated
Describes animals that have been trained or bred to live or work alongside humans. Many types of dog are domesticated.

Droppings
Waste produced by animals, such as birds or rodents.

Fish
Cold-blooded animals that live in water. They breathe through gills, and have fins to help them swim. A shark is a type of fish.

Freshwater
The water from rain or snow that flows in rivers and lakes. It is not salty like seawater.

Grazer
A large animal that feeds mainly on grass. Zebras are grazers.

Habitat
The natural environment where an animal or plant lives.

Hibernation
A deep sleep that some animals go into in winter. They usually find a warm, safe place where they sleep until spring, when food is available again.

Island
An area of land that is surrounded by water. Australia is an island.

Mammal
A type of animal that produces milk to feed its babies. Humans and cats are both mammals.

Marine
Describes animals and plants that live in the sea.

Marsupial
A type of mammal where the mother has a special pouch to carry her young until they have developed properly.

Migration
Journeys that some animals make from one place to another, usually to find food, a warmer climate, or a safe place to have their young.

Mollusk
One of a group of animals that have shells. Snails and mussels are mollusks.

Nectar
A sweet syrup that flowers make to attract insects, such as bees. In return, bees help plants reproduce (make new plants).

Nocturnal
Describes animals that are most active during the night. Badgers are nocturnal.

Ocean
A very large sea. There are five oceans on Earth: the Atlantic, Arctic, Indian, Pacific, and Southern.

Polar regions
The areas of land or sea around the North and South poles.

Predator
Describes an animal that hunts other animals for food. Wolves and sharks are both predators.

Prey
Describes an animal that is hunted by another for food. Worms are the prey of moles and badgers.

Primate
One of a group of mammals with a large brain, and hands and feet that can grasp. Monkeys are primates.

Reptile
One of a group of cold-blooded animals that are covered with scales or bony armor. Snakes are reptiles.

Rodent
One of a group of animals with extra-strong front teeth for gnawing. Beavers are rodents.

Scavenger
An animal that feeds on the dead bodies of other animals. Vultures are scavengers.

School
A large number of fish swimming together.

Species
A group of animals of the same type, which share the same characteristics.

Taiga
Cold forests of evergreen conifer trees near the Arctic region.

Venomous
Describes an animal that uses poisonous bites or stings to capture prey or fight enemies.

INDEX